# Stress Free Living

## Is it possible or just a dream?

Thomas A. Mayberry

# DEDICATION

To the memory of

## Steffanie Ann Leonard

Nov. 1, 1982 – Feb. 22, 2012

We all can learn from her carefree living. She never stressed over what the future had in store for her. Steffanie lived in the moment. Her life was tragically taken by a drunk driver going the wrong way on the highway. She is truly missed but she touched so many lives.

# SPECIAL THANKS

I could never accomplish writing a book by myself. I want to thank my sister, Mary, for the time that she put in proofreading my work. I had read the book numerous times but what she pointed out looked so obvious, but I had missed. She also gave me the emotional support to share more about my life so that it may help others.

I cannot say enough about the Christian fellowship that I have with members of Hermitage United Methodist church and the Shema Sunday school class. You have played a bigger role in my life than you ever have known.

Thank you to Marti and Jennifer Leonard for the foreword to this book. As mother and sister of Steffanie Leonard, it was hard for you to put into words what she meant to you. Steffanie can be an inspiration to all of us.

# FOREWORD

From the moment Steffanie took her first breath, she embodied a stress free lifestyle. She knew no boundaries and she had no limits. Whether climbing out of her baby bed at 16 months, joining the boys wrestling team in middle school, or traveling to destinations unknown Steffanie lived life with gusto and abandon. She never concerned herself with what others thought or said instead she focused on what adventure would call her name next. She didn't stress about the little things that trip so many of us up, but instead looked at the big picture of what was truly important: relationships with family and friends. Steffanie pushed each of us to live our lives to the fullest and encouraged us to never let the thoughts of the world stand in our way.

Tragically Steffanie's life was cut short on February 22, 2012 when a drunk driver hit her head on while Steffanie traveled to work. It is a day I will never forget. Each moment after I have asked myself constantly how I can honor Steffanie's memory. What can I do to keep her spirit alive and how would she want each of us to remember her. I have come to the conclusion that she would ask us to live our lives with joy. Seek each day to live life to the fullest and don't let anyone or anything hold us back. Focus on those around us and invest our lives in them. Make sure our family and friends never doubt our love for them. Find ways to bring happiness to each person that crosses our paths. Be sunshine in the darkness. Live in the present, move on from the past, and don't worry about the future. Just breathe, and live, and keep moving forward.

I promise to do just that Motormouth. Love you forever.

Jenn

My daughter, Steffanie Ann, made her presence known beginning at birth. Weighing in at almost "10" lb. and "2" feet in length, she was making the statement, "Here I am." Steffanie showed no fear....she wanted to experience all of life to the fullest. In doing this, she did it with excitement and the quest to learn something about everything. Steffanie had the ability to participate in a conversation on any subject with any person because she was always on a quest for more knowledge. She was outspoken, and at the same time, had a gentleness that touched all who came into contact with her. The day Steffanie lost her life, she began a new life....experiencing the wonders of Heaven. My heart is heavy with the loss of my daughter, yet I pledge to live life to the fullest, committing to learn something new each day and if there is no path to a new experience, than I will forge a path......all in honor of Steffanie Ann Leonard. I thank my daughter for all she taught me and the legacy she has left.

I love you, Steffanie Ann "Motormouth" Leonard,

Mom

# Table of Contents

# Introduction

I have been asked by many of my friends how I picked stress management as the topic for my second book. I primarily have focused my attention on how to lead people. Stress management has an impact on the way that you lead people more than you think. It is crucial to create a stress free work environment to be able to get more out of your team. I enjoy watching sports. I see many athletes that can stay calm in pressure situations and lead their teams to victory. At the same time we see other teams that fall apart due to the stress and ultimately lose.

This same approach can be applied to all aspects of your life that you are a leader. I have been blessed with the ability to stay calm and relaxed in most areas of my life. I have also seen the other end of the spectrum of stress in my life. Writing this book has opened my eyes to the area of my life that I was not completely honest with myself as to my stress level. I am going to share some stress reducing techniques with you throughout this book. If it came down to just using techniques, though, we would all be living stress free. You need to approach stress management with the right attitude.

I apply a Christian approach to stress management, as I do in most areas of my life. This has made a huge impact in my capability to control my stress level. When I bottomed out in stress a number of years ago, it was my Christian fellowship that pulled me out of it. I have grown closer in my walk with God and see the difference it has made in my ability to handle stress.

Use this book as a tool. Refer back to it on a regular basis when you find yourself needing that extra support in situations. This book will not change your life overnight. It is a journey that we are taking. This book will help you along in your journey to take control over your stress.

Thomas

# 1

# Is it Possible or just a Dream?

Is your goal to become stress free? Is it really possible? Can you live your life without any stress? We live in a world surrounded by stressful situations. Some of these situations we have control over and we can dictate how much stress we allow. In other situations, we do not have control over what happens. In this case we still need to control how much we allow it to increase our stress level.

Some say that it is not possible to live without stress. The main purpose of this book is to help you acknowledge and manage your stress. You should be able to control the stress factors in your life so that they do not control you. I repeat that you may not be able to control what happens in all situations. You can, however, be aware of your stress level and maintain control over it. You need to be able to tell the signs of stress so that you can react and relax.

Are you one of those people that others feel never gets "worked up" over anything? Your friends and co-workers believe that nothing ever bothers you.

This is great if not only that is what shows on the outside, but is also the reality on the inside. If you have that persona on the outside, but inside you are holding in stress, this is a recipe for failure. You have to admit to yourself that you have that stress and address it.

Stress is a normal physical response to events that make you feel threatened or completely go differently than planned. When you sense danger – whether it's real or imagined – the body's defenses kick into high gear in a rapid, automatic process known as the "fight or flight" reaction. I see this in my cat every day. I recently painted my bedroom. The cat used to stroll in there without a care in the world. Now as soon as she gets near the room, she puts her guard up. She is very observant to the things around her. It is almost to the point of paranoia. If there is any sound or if she senses movement out of her peripheral vision, she jumps back and sometimes flees the room.

This response is the body's way of protecting you. In a way, it keeps you focused and alert to everything around you. It prepares you for potential danger so that you can react quickly. It could, in some instances, save your life. This fight or flight response to stress does not necessarily mean that your life is in danger. Imagine sitting in the audience of a presentation at work and suddenly you are asked to come up to the front and give a short presentation about your recent successes. You obviously know the information well, but what if you are scared to death of speaking in front of an audience. Your mind starts telling you to figure out a way to get out of it or just fight through it. Not everyone is comfortable in front of a group and asked to speak to them. I enjoy this type of setting, but dread going to a networking event where I need to strike up a conversation with strangers. Everyone has situations in their life's that will trigger this fight or flight response.

Not all stress is overwhelming. Some stress is productive. I am not talking about big amounts of stress. If you let your stress get out of control, you lose the effect. This smaller level of stress is what helps my sons stay up late to study for their next college exam. It can help you stay focused on the task at hand. I have started to exercise more. I am now jogging on a regular basis and lifting weights at the gym. Before I run, I need to stretch out my muscles so that they are more flexible and can handle more of the strain that I put on them. This stretching is putting small amounts of stress to the muscles. When lifting weights, you take the same type of approach to be able to build up your muscles. You actually create small tears in the

3

muscle tissues that cause the muscle to grow during the healing process.

Stress in smaller doses is a good thing. Carrying stress too far will have an impact on your health, your approach to life and your relationships with co-workers, friends and family. Maybe your goal should be to have a healthy controllable amount of stress in your life. The main focus should be on your ability to control your stress levels.

By having the ability to control the stress in your life, you can have a much more relaxed and satisfying environment. This, in turn, affects those around you and that atmosphere will spread.

I consider it to be especially important when you are leading a team. The more you are in control of the environment that your team is working in, the more productive they will be. In this book, I will guide you through your own self development so that those around you will see a difference and be impacted by it.

# 2

# Take the First Step

The first step to being able to control your stress is to realize what stress does to your body. You need to be more attentive to the signs of your growing stress levels. This will give you the ability to take control of the situation much sooner. My mom is diabetic and has been for over 50 years. She has to be very "in tune" with what her body is telling her in regards to her blood sugar levels. If she does not see the signs soon enough to react, it is much harder to get it back under control.

Part of this knowledge comes with experience. Everybody processes their diets differently and she needed to understand more how her body reacts to different foods. She also has had regular checkups with the doctors that have coached her along the way. It is the same principle in controlling your stress. You need to have coaching from people that can teach you the signs of stress. You can learn what your approach to stressful situations is.

Do you know how you react to stress? Are you consistent with your response to stressful situations? Psychologist Connie Lillas used a driving analogy to describe the three most common ways people respond when they're overwhelmed by stress:

**Foot on the gas** – An angry or agitated stress response. You're heated, keyed up, overly emotional, and unable to sit still.

**Foot on the brake** – A withdrawn or depressed stress response. You shut down, space out, and show very little energy or emotion.

**Foot on both** – A tense and frozen stress response. You "freeze" under pressure and can't do anything. You look paralyzed, but under the surface you're extremely agitated.

I know some people that have their foot on the gas. I can hear them now as they are reading this saying that I am talking about them again. That is a good sign, because it means that they understand how their body reacts to stress. You have to understand what is going on in your body to be able to get more control in situations that arise. This is the first step to getting control over it.

I teach people how to create a stress free work environment. The main way that you can reduce the stress on your team is to take control of your own stress. If you get overly worked up and angry, this will take away from the team environment that you are trying to build up. You need to be aware of how your stress affects your conversations with those around you.

I, personally, get a little withdrawn. I tend to have my foot on the brake pedal. I do not really want to talk to anyone about it. I do not want them to see my stress. I see it as a sense of weakness on my part and do not want it to affect those around me. I want to portray an image of never letting anything get to me. I have seen a great improvement in my ability to control stress over the past 5-10 years. This has actually been easier the more that my faith in God has grown. As my faith grows and I put into practice what I have read in the Bible, I experience less stress.

You do not normally spot the ones that have their foot on both the gas pedal and the brakes. They tend to keep the agitated side to themselves, so are harder to read. You know who you are, though. I had a manager work for me that was extremely organized. Her whole day was plotted out and her team almost ran on autopilot. The problem was what would happen when something did not go as planned. At that point, she would freeze up. It was as if she would throw up her hands and say, "I give up." She would think that she could not get everything accomplished that she wanted to do. I would see this in her frustration and ask her if I could take one project off of her plate. Immediately she realized that she was not as far off of her plan as she thought that she was. We need to learn the personalities of our co-workers and friends. As we see the signs of stress in their lives, we need to offer support in ways that can assist them in reducing their stress.

Think about yourself. How do you react to stress? Are you aware of how your body is affected? I would like you to start thinking about the kinds of things that cause stress in your life.

Let's look at some of the warning signs and symptoms of stress. The following table lists some of the common warning signs and symptoms of stress. What do you see in yourself? Think of a stressful situation in the past couple of weeks. Did you experience any of these?

As I write this, I have a co-worker that is currently trying to quit smoking after 30 years. I have seen the signs of stress in her over the past couple of weeks.  She is trying her best to take control of the situation.   Here are some of the symptoms that people in stressful situations experience.   I have seen some of these symptoms in her.

## *Moodiness*

We see this in our friends, co-workers and family all the time.  Have you thought about the fact that it may be the outward sign of their stress level?   As our stress level goes up, we tend to have mood swings.  Your mood is going to change somewhat through the day.  The different activities that you get involved in are going to change your mood. Spending time with friends might raise your spirits after work.  You may be intensely focused after a manager meeting and barely acknowledge someone who you pass in the hallway.

This is just a natural part of being human.   The moodiness that I am talking about is when you expressing moods that are not "normal" for you. You are in those settings that normally make you very happy and social and you are quiet and to yourself.  You do not interact with others in the way that they are used to you acting.

## Short temper

This warning sign stands out more than some of the others. Little things begin to bother us and we lash out. We do not mean to, but we cannot control it. Many times we see what we are doing but cannot control ourselves. We tend to get impatient and it triggers our anger. We want things to go our way even more so than we normally do. Later we tend to apologize for our behavior. We do not want to express this temper with our friends and co-workers. It just happens. It is the stress that is getting to us.

## Agitation

Our temper is coming from being agitated. We get frustrated over more things than normal. It may be that everything is not going the way that we planned it. We want to be in control all the time and when this control slips from us, we get agitated. We also tend to let little things bother us. This may be someone tapping their fingers on the table to a song that they are listening to. It may be someone that chews with their mouth open. We get so upset over these things. When we are not stressed, we can tolerate more things that people do.

## Inability to concentrate

I get easily distracted by what is bothering me. I cannot concentrate on the task that is front of me. My mind keeps wandering back to what is causing my stress. Part of stress management is to be able to temporarily block out those thoughts. It is not easy. We almost get obsessed with what is bothering us. I know that you have heard people say to leave your problems at home when you go to work. Also, we are told to leave work at work and not bring it home with us. Our spouse and children do not want to hear about what is bugging us at work.

The reason that we need to try to do this is because we need to concentrate on our family when we are at home. You will see this concentration go down when you are stressed. The same thing happens when you are at work and things that are stressing you in your personal life are on your mind at work. You need to be more aware of some of these symptoms of stress so that you can address them.

## Not having a positive outlook

As our stress level goes up, our positive outlook goes down. We start to view more of the negative things about a situation. Our whole attitude changes when this happens. Frustration sets in and you start believing that things will not get better. This starts to build up and it gets tougher to change it back to a positive attitude. Awareness is the key. Most of the things that we worry and stress about never happen. In some cases, the situation gets worse because we are stressed about it and we are not taking care of the things that we do have control over. We need to decide in our minds that things are going to turn to the positive. This leads to your overall happiness.

## General unhappiness

We get discouraged and sad. This is the start down the path to depression. You need to recognize this happening to be able to address it. It starts with stress. The stress levels that we have tend to wear on us. The more that we try to hide from our true feelings, the worse they become. As discussed earlier, we get frustrated and start to see an attitude change to the negative. It is very hard to be happy when you have a negative attitude. All of these symptoms feed off of each other and our stress continues to build.

Each of us knows what makes us happy. There are things that you can add into your week to help your mood. The key is to schedule these in. Most of these are the stress relievers that I discuss throughout this book.

## Memory problems

As your stress level rises, you get more and more things on your mind. Our minds can only process one thought at a time. People say that they are very good at multi-tasking. What they are actually good at is starting and stopping tasks and remembering where they left off. As we bounce back and forth between everything going on, it is easy to start forgetting things. We start to lose our concentration. We cannot keep track of everything the way that we normally can. If you see your stress level going up, it may be necessary for you to write things down more often. I see myself doing this on a regular basis. I have realized that a simple task is easily remembered when I am calm and relaxed. The more stress that I have, I know that the more apt I am to forget things. Even simple things can slip by me when I am stressed over things.

My kids have given me a hard time over the years because I almost always carried a pen in my pocket. Even on my days off. On the surface, it sounds like a stupid habit. This allowed me to write notes to myself as things come up that I need to remember. I also have noticed that as my stress levels go down, I tend to not have that pen with me. I know that it is not a coincidence.

## Aches and pains

Stress has numerous effects on our health. Sometimes it causes our lifestyles to change some. We may not be as active as when we are relaxed. We are stressed from work and come home and do not want to do anything. Then, when we do get out being active again, we are not in as good of shape. It may be that we just become more aware of the aches and pains of our bodies. When you get frustrated with things going on in your life and your attitude starts to turn, you are looking for things to get upset about. You start to notice the negatives things going on with your body.

## Stomach and digestive issues

I tend to keep the company in business that sells medicines for these issues. I can blame it on peppers and onions as much as I want, but stress plays a factor in many situations as well as my diet. I tend to wake up in the middle of the night with an upset stomach. Acid has built up and I take a pill and try to get back to sleep. I also realize while I am awake at this point about the things during the day that need to get done or the negative things that are on my mind. Different people react to stress by doing different things and having different symptoms. I know firsthand that I fall into some of these behaviors. Are you starting to recognize the symptoms of your stress?

## Emotional eating

So many people fall into this category. At the time that it is happening, you may not even be aware of it. If you enjoy eating, it is easy to fall into this problem. Eating makes you feel good, so you do it to mask the stress. My weight has gone up and down over the years. I am not talking about 5-10 lbs. at a time. I see swings of 30, 40, 50 lbs or more at a time. I do not see it at the time, but looking back, I can tie a lot of it to stress. As we try to get control over our stress, a key is healthy eating. Just an occasional change in our diet will not get us there. We need to have a lifestyle change.

When I was in charge of the cafeteria and catering department in our division, I had my stressful times. There was so much that I wanted to get done throughout the day that I would not stop for lunch.

I had access to food at each of my stops, so it was easy to get something to go and eat while driving down the road. Now I realized that I could not eat a salad or a healthy entrée and vegetables while driving a car. The easiest food for this was from the short order grill. Burgers, fries and other fried foods became a staple of my diet. My weight started to climb again.

I wish that I had a magic wand to help get rid of stress, but it is not always easy. It takes effort on your part. Being aware of how you react to stress, especially in the area of eating, will help you to control this reaction leading to a healthier lifestyle.

## Not getting enough sleep

This is typically not because you do not go to bed early enough to get enough sleep. It is because you do not get long enough stretches of good sleep. You toss and turn trying to fall asleep and then wake up off and on throughout the night because your mind is racing over what is causing the stress. As I mentioned earlier, in my case, the stress also causes digestive issues. This leads to breaks in my sleep throughout the night. Your healthy eating habits can play a factor in your sleep habits. Do you see the pattern that so many of these symptoms are tied together as well as the things that you do to take control of your stress? You need to be aware that many of the areas that you change in your lifestyle to control stress play a factor on each other.

## Avoiding others

All you can think about is "Leave me alone." It may be because you are agitated. You do not want to talk about your stress and just want some "alone time". Making time to be alone is not a bad thing. Everyone needs time to themselves. You need to be aware of why you want time to yourself. Is it that you are trying to get away from the things that are stressing you? Stress will cause you to do this.

Your alone time should be scheduled for the stress reducing activities of your life. Don't just go home from work and sit on the couch and mope about how bad you have it. Find an activity that reminds you about how good you have it.

## Smoking cigarettes

Most people are aware of the dangers of smoking. Smoking may relax the mind, most likely, because nicotine triggers the release of pleasant brain chemicals like norepinephrine and beta-endorphins. Ironically, while smoking makes people feel calmer, it actually puts physical stress on their bodies because nicotine is a stimulant. Smoking raises a person's heart rate and causes muscle tension. The blood vessels constrict, depriving the body and brain of oxygen. I am not going to harp on cigarette smoking because I have heard that it is not an easy addiction to quit. I do want you to realize the impact that it has on your stress level.

## *Drinking alcohol*

Some people use alcohol to relax after a hectic and stressful day. In moderation, this may help. What begins to happen is that you start to rely on the alcohol to "calm your nerves". It is an addiction that builds up without your awareness. You would be better off to not start using alcohol as a stress reliever.

Be aware of your habits. Are they changing and involving the drinking of alcohol more often? It is a sign of your increased stress levels that you need to address. Some people associate drinking with having a good time with friends. Most of these activities with friends can be just as enjoyable without drinking.

As we get older, many of us tell others that those drinking and partying days are way behind us. We cannot act like college students anymore. Others take longer to mature and take responsibility for their actions. This is why we have so many people killed by drunk drivers every year. The first step may be to still be friends with these people but to not participate in all of the activities that put pressure on you to drink with them.

## Yelling or being very abrupt with co-workers, peers and family

This goes back to being agitated. You start to take your frustrations out on the people around you. Have you worked with someone that is having a bad day and everyone knows to just leave them alone? Have you asked each other "What is wrong with them?" It is probably the stress that is getting to them. We have to be more aware of the fact that we are doing that. It will bring more awareness to the stress level that we have. It is one of the signals that tell us to use one, or more, of our stress relieving activities.

## Decreased productivity

I wrote earlier about the fact that we lose our concentration. With this, comes a decrease in our productivity. We cannot stay on task because our mind keeps going back to what we are stressing over. Also, we tend to bounce from project to project, trying to do too many things at once. In the end, we do not get as much done. This happens to me at work sometimes.

My desk becomes covered up with papers tied to different projects. I start working on one project and before it is through, I have a manager come in and give me another project. Instead of telling them, that it will be awhile before I can help them, I stop what I am doing and go on ahead and finish their need. I would be much more productive to finish what I was working on and then take care of the manager's need. The stress that I put on myself to take care of everyone else is what makes me be very unproductive on my own projects.

You are not alone in these areas of stress and how they affect us. All of your friends, family and co-workers have had stressful situations in their lives. Open up to them and let them coach and guide you through it. Just talking about it helps to reduce some of the stress in situations. As you talk to others, they will probably be able to share some ideas of how to improve the situation. We learn from our own mistakes and behaviors, so we can use these learning situations to coach others through the tough times.

These are some of the common signs of stress and their affects on you. Think back over the past few months of when you were in stressful situations. Did you see some of these affects in yourself? Going forward, you need to be attentive to when these things are affecting you. By doing this, you will spot the stress before it gets out of control.

# 3

# A Living Example

As I told you earlier, I personally, get a little withdrawn. I tend to have my foot on the brake pedal. I used to be very much withdrawn and I did not really want to talk to anyone about my stress. I did not want them to see my stress. As my faith grows and I put into practice what I read in the Bible, the less stress that I experience.

*God was not ready for me yet. He still had plans for me.*

I used to not be this way. For years, I was very aggressive in my approach to my career. I was determined to move up the corporate ladder no matter what the cost. I had gone through a divorce already and was going down the same path again. I had a lot of stress in my life and would not share it with anyone. I would put on a false front at work and around friends and family. They continued to see me as being very "laid back". When we moved to Tennessee in 1996, I realized that I had just about cost myself another marriage and had not been there for my kids. My oldest son was just starting school. I had to change my ways, or I was going to have a disaster on my hands.

I switched companies and found a job in restaurant management that was Monday through Friday, mostly daytime hours. I got active with my sons and the sports that they played at that age. We joined a bowling league for families so that we would have regularly scheduled family time. I coached little league baseball. On the outside, we were beginning to look like the model family again. We bought a house and got a dog. Life was good on the surface.

Over the next several years, we started to struggle financially. I had taken a pay cut to get better hours with my new job. My wife wanted to go back to school to get a degree, so she started taking a class each semester. She was working two jobs and I picked up a second job, but it was getting harder to juggle everything. During my full-time job, I was doing a lot of catering for factories that operated three shifts. There were many 20 hour work days with trying to keep up a part-time job as well as my full time career.

Around the fall of 2004, I had a rude awakening that my marriage was shattered. It had hit rock bottom. My stress got the best of me. I spiraled into a state of depression. I continued to portray that false front to family and friends. We were already on the verge of bankruptcy and got to the point where the only way that we could save the house would be to file. The holidays were rough on me since I was not happy. The catering part of my job was booming more than ever, so the hours were intense and I was still working 15 hours a week at the mall job. I was a wreck.

New Years Day came and my wife and kids went to see one of her friends for the afternoon and evening. I stayed home because I got the impression that she did not want me along with them. By mid-afternoon, I had come to the conclusion that I could not take any more of this. I decided that suicide was my only solution. I went out to the garage and hooked up a hose to the exhaust of the car and fed it into the back seat window. I started up the car and started to pray. I asked God to forgive me for all that I had done wrong. I had not been the husband and father that I should have been. I wanted the everlasting life that He had promised me and I was eager to get to Heaven where all of my suffering would end. I started to cry immensely.

God was not ready for me yet. He still had plans for me. At that moment, the hose popped out of the window. I knew immediately that my suicide was not meant to be. It was God that pulled the hose out of the window. I unhooked the hose from the exhaust and aired out the car and garage. After a brief time in the house, I decided to take myself to the doctor's office for help.

I told him that I had thoughts of suicide. I was too embarrassed to tell him that I had actually attempted it. I was taken to the hospital for further observation and counseling. My wife had to come back early from her friend's house to pick me up. They would not let me drive myself under the circumstances. I told her that I had thoughts of suicide, but never told her that I had attempted it. She was upset that her plans were changed. As she told me, if I had told the doctor that I was depressed and not mentioned the word suicide, I could have driven myself home. I was ashamed that I even had those thoughts, so never told her what I had actually done.

I went to Sunday school that weekend and a dear friend came to me before class and said "I got an e-mail from you that had prayer request in the subject line but nothing in the body of the e-mail." She asked me if the body of the e-mail accidentally got erased. I told her that I had not sent it. I started to weep as I realized that God had sent her to comfort me. I shared my struggles in life with her and how devastated I was that my marriage was in shambles. That was the day that I really became aware of my walk with Christ. Sure, we have had conversations over the years through prayer. He was with me all the time and I did not really notice. I just had not been aware of how much He was taking care of me if I would let Him.

I wanted to share this story, even though it has been hard to put on paper. It is part of my healing process, but you need to learn from it as I have. Depression is one of the side effects of stress that can really build up over time. Be aware of your friends and family and if you see any changes in their behavior. I am not by any means an expert on suicide. I can only share what my feelings are from my perspective.

Just show love and comfort to those that you know are going through an emotionally stressful time. Give them opportunities to vent their frustrations and just be there to listen. Do not be judgmental or try to tell them to make themselves less depressed. Realize that they may not want to share what is bothering them, but that does not mean that they do not appreciate your concern. It may be as simple as taking someone out to lunch or dinner. If they are not interested, just call them on the phone regularly to let them talk through what is on their mind.

Do not just ignore them and wait for them to get better. You need to keep the communication flowing. It could be in the form of short e-mails, text messages, forwarding a joke to give them a smile. Do not always expect answers to these communications, but realize that they are appreciated by the one that is going through the tough time in their life.

Many people with depression tend to isolate themselves from others. They will not seek out social activities. Do not pressure them to get out and do things. For them to just know that they have opportunities to socialize helps their mental state. Offering to pray for someone shows that you care about their wellbeing. You do not need to know all of the details of their situation. They may not want to share it with you.

Your prayer should consist of asking God to step into their life and help them along the way. Remember that you are praying for God's will to be done and not what you want to happen. You pray that God will comfort them and get them through the current situations in their lives. Sometimes it is meant to be for them to struggle. It may be years later that they realize why they had to endure the current situation. The biggest thing is to just show that you love them and care enough about them to help them through the tough times.

If my friend had approached me a week before that, maybe I would have opened up and never went down that path. I am ashamed of what I did that day in the garage. This is the main reason that I have never shared this with family members over the years. Anyone who knows me well knows that I do not believe in coincidences and I now know that God is always working His will in my life. I believe that He let me go down that path and bottom out. That was the only way that He could get through to me about what was truly important in life.

Some people have the misconception that once you become a Christian that you will have a perfect life and nothing wrong will happen. You will still have the struggles that others are having. The difference is that you will have God helping you through those tough times. From that point forward, I have never had thoughts of suicide again. I wanted to share my story to let others learn from it. Both from the aspect of the person with severe stress and from the view point of those around them that can help.

If you are having thoughts of suicide, please seek help. This can be in the form of going to a counselor to help guide you through the situation. Talk to your pastor for spiritual guidance and prayer. You may need medical attention as well to be put on an anti-depression medicine until you stabilize. There are many avenues available to you.

I was too ashamed of my situation and waited too long to seek help. I encourage you to take care of yourself first. You cannot help those around you in your family if you do not put enough effort into your own well-being.

# 4

## It's all about the Attitude

I have noticed over the years that different people have different tolerance levels of the main things in life that stress us.  I personally have been on the lower level of the scale when it comes to being "stressed out" over the past few years.  I just do not let a lot of things bother me anymore.  As I am writing this chapter, my air conditioner is broken at my house.  It has been down for two and a half weeks.  This is one of the hottest Junes in history for Nashville.  The temperatures have been around 100 degrees most days lately.

When it first went out, I prayed to God that He figure out a way to get it replaced.  God has always provided for me and I know that He always will.  In the letter to the Philippians, Paul wrote "Don't worry about anything; instead, pray about everything. Tell God what you need, and thank him for all he has done."  I am going through a divorce, so money is very tight.   I could not afford a replacement unit even though that would probably be the best case scenario for long range planning.

God however was going to take care of my needs and not necessarily my wants.

I have explored so many different options including financing with a bank and having a friend loan me money but nothing felt right. The temperature kept going up. It is close to 100 degrees outside today. Immediately after hearing about my crisis, a friend loaned me some window air conditioner units. That has been a great temporary fix, but did not solve my long term need. I struggled to get a new unit financed without paying outrageous interest rates. All along, I kept praying that God would take care of me and thanked Him again for always providing for my needs.

Later this week, I will have the condenser replaced and will be sitting in comfort again. I will not owe any money long term due to an unexpected bonus check from work. Once again, God has provided for me. I could have stressed over it as the heat went up, but I chose not to. I chose to have the faith that everything would work out. It is all about the attitude.

I have a dinner party scheduled at my house for 12 people this weekend. I was speaking to one of the guests, a neighbor of mine, about my dilemma with the air conditioner. He told me that if I needed to move the dinner to his house at the last minute, I could. Once again, God is providing for me. I told him that I had faith that it would all come together in time for the dinner. Looking back at it afterwards, everything was great for the dinner. It was a way to raise money for my church's Habitat for Humanity build project later in the fall. We enjoyed the Christian fellowship and delicious food that evening. A couple extra fans in the area helped keep the temperature in a comfortable range. It just proved to me that I never had to stress over the situation.

We need to have the ability to pray to God and let Him take care of us. This attitude is reflected in the *Serenity Prayer,* which has been adopted and used by many members of 12 step groups. Praying it helps you deal with the stress in your life.

*God, give me grace to accept with serenity, the things that cannot be changed, Courage to change the things which should be changed, and the Wisdom to distinguish the one from the other.*

The first written form of this was in a sermon by Reinhold Niebuhr in 1943. These are powerful words that when applied to your life can make a difference in your stress level. Everyone will be put in stressful situations. It is your approach to these situations that dictates your stress level. I ask people all the time why they stress over things that they cannot control. It is not going to change them. The only thing that happens when you stress over items that are out of your control is that you may affect things that you do have control over. You lose focus on what you can handle by stressing over things that you cannot change.

I remember catering for about a hundred twenty people in downtown Nashville. It was a summer afternoon. I had a couple of people working with me. We brought in all our supplies. We were catering on the plaza in front of one of the high-rise office buildings. We were aiming for an 11:00 serving time and got there in plenty of time. I do not like to get stressed out over being late so do not wait until last minute to get someplace.

Are you the type of person that has your daily commute timed down to the minute? You know exactly when you have to leave your house so you can clock in right at the time to start work. You have that meeting with a client across town and you know that it will take twenty minutes to get their but you don't leave the office until twenty minutes before your appointment. That is not me. Trust me, I have many faults. Timeliness, though, is normally not one of them.

As I was working to get the line set up. I had one of my coworkers go to the truck for the food and supplies. He tried to make as few trips as possible. He was trying to be very efficient. This is normally a good trait. I noticed what looked like an attempt to maximize the amount of stuff he could put on the cart. He hit the curb a little bit more force than I guess he thought that he was hitting it to get up onto the sidewalk. Let me point out, that at the top of this cart, was a five gallon igloo dispenser filled with hot cheese sauce. It was an easy way to carry it. It keeps it nice and hot and prevents it from running all over the place. Guess what hit the ground? It was the five gallons of melted cheese sauce. It went all over the edge of the sidewalk and just into the street. To add to the suspense, was that the spilled cheese sauce was about 15ft. away from the valet parking of a major hotel. It is one of the nicest hotels in Nashville. Do you think I was stressed?

You are saying to yourself, "this could cause a lot of stress." I would take the approach that I am only going to stress over what I can control and not what is not under my control. At this point in time there was nothing that I could do to make the cheese sauce disappear from that street. I had to give up control of that particular situation. But I was not about to lose control over my vision. Remember, my vision was to give a great catering experience to my clients.

I immediately picked up the phone and contacted one of my managers at the nearest kitchen to where we were catering. I explained to her that I would talk to her later about what had happened but what I needed her to do now was to start preparing more cheese sauce. I had to tell her that there was no time to talk about it. I was pushing the limits as far as time to get the catering ready and that if the water was not already on the burner heating up, she needed to take care of that first.

I then turned to the employee that spilled the cheese sauce and said that he needed to quickly try to scoop up off the ground as much as he could and put in a container and put it on the truck. Do not worry about cleaning it up all the way, just get the bulk of it off the ground and come finish helping to set up the serving line. I took control of the situation at hand and did not let it control me.

The manager showed up, with five minutes to spare, with more cheese sauce that we put on the line. The client never knew what we went through to pull off the catering. Now I know if that you're wondering what happened to the cheese sauce.

I glanced over, during the middle of the catering, back to the street. I saw the valet attendants at the hotel across the street with buckets of water washing the cheese sauce down the street. I think back of the priorities that I had. I put my tasks in the "must do" and the "should do" categories. The "must do" is that I needed to have an exceptional catering experience for my clients. The "should do", in this case, is keep that street clean and not spill cheese sauce everywhere. I accomplished my "must do."

You have to have an **optimistic attitude** to help you in potentially stressful situations. Sometimes we become what we believe is true. We bring on bad things in our lives because we do not feel that we have a choice to defend ourselves from it. This summer we had the opportunity to watch the athletes compete in the Olympic games. There were so many stories about athletes that have overcome serious injuries. It could have been easy for them to say to themselves that they have bad luck and use this as an excuse to give up trying. Instead, they believed in their hearts that they were one of the best in their sport and pushed through it. They had the positive attitude that they would heal and be ready for the competition.

Too often, we give up. We do not give it the extra effort needed to succeed because we believe that something else will go wrong next. We need to change our belief to one of "everything is possible if we just have faith in the outcome." Here is a good example of where an optimistic attitude kept me from experiencing extra stress in a tough situation.

I was having a conversation with a co-worker last week about the use of debit and credit cards for purchases on the internet. She worries that someone will steal her information. I told her that I do not worry about it at all. I explained that I do not feel that it could never happen to me. I believe in being careful, but I also realize that thieves are very good and there is always that possibility that they can get my debit and credit card numbers and use them.

I told her that I look at the worst case scenario and realize that I may be inconvenienced short term with the loss of money if they get money out of my checking account. Eventually, the bank would credit me back the funds, because I will not be held responsible for fraudulent charges. Also, I know that God has always provided for my needs (not necessarily my wants) and always will.

## Philippians 4:19 (NIV)

*And my God will meet all your needs according to his glorious riches in Christ Jesus.*

Later on that night, I got a phone call from my bank asking if I was in California pulling out money from ATMs. There had been close to $600 in transactions in a short period of time. I explained that I did not do these transactions. He proceeded to cancel my debit card and order me a new one. The next day I had to go to the bank to fill out a report to deny the charges and request a refund. I was told that it could take up to two weeks to get my money back. OK, maybe now I need to watch what I talk about at work. Did I jinx myself?

If I did not have the positive attitude going into this experience, I would have experienced a huge amount of stress. I definitely could not afford to lose $600. As I said earlier, money has been tight. My faith in God to provide for my needs, allowed me to get through this experience with no stress at all.

About a week later, the bank has put the money back into my account. How would have you handled the situation? Would you stay positive, or would your stress level escalate out of control?

This same approach can be applied to all aspects of your life. So many people worry about what could possibly go wrong. There is nothing wrong with thinking about what could go wrong so that you have back up plans if needed. Bad things happen to everyone. We have had this discussion in our Sunday school class on numerous occasions. Some people think that if you are a Christian that God is going to prevent all bad things from happening to you. This is not the case. God will be there by your side to walk with you through all areas of your life. He will be there through the good times and through your struggles. I find that my faith grows more through the struggles because it makes me more aware of His presence and how He is helping me handle those situations.

If you really put things into perspective, the worst case scenario is not really as bad as we think it is. Remember, is it a "want" or a "need"? It is all in the attitude.

Your **close friends and family** will also give you strength in the potential stressful situations. Rely on them and share your concerns with them. They can give you comfort and strength. I regularly have long conversations with my best friend. We share our struggles and help each other put things into perspective. We comfort each other through the tough times. Normally it is just being a good listener that helps heal what is bothering the other person. The more that you isolate yourself from others effects the situation and the stress will build up inside of you and you lose control of your stress level. Just talking about it provides comfort. Your close friends and family should know you enough to be able to guide you through the situation.

I am very involved with a Sunday school class at my church. At the end of class each week, we allow time to discuss our praises and prayer concerns. I continue to praise God each week for how he answered our prayers from the week before. Having fellow Christian friends to lean on during times of stress is a blessing. The comforting that they provide is priceless. I have also had friends ask for prayers about a situation and someone in the room knows someone in that field of expertise that can help them through it. I do not believe that it is a coincidence.

You need to have the full experience of your Christian faith. It is not enough to just attend church regularly or to just read the Bible each day and not attend church. Imagine it as a choice in a restaurant.

If you were given the choice of ordering one item, ala carte', or being able to get a four course meal, you would probably go for the full meal. After having the complete meal, you would have a full range of your needs met and have a very satisfying experience.

You need to put your Christian faith in this same perspective. The reason that this is important is that the more that you apply your faith into your personal and work environment, the less stressful and more successful you will be. This is not accomplished by taking the ala carte' approach to your spiritual growth. I think of those that attend church just on Christmas and Easter. They are only getting an appetizer.

I have seen people that seem to be more faithful to God and do not attend church regularly and some that attend a lot, but do not apply any of the principles to their lives. That is why I propose going for the full meal. Our church offers many adult

Sunday school class options. It is the opportunity to study God's word and how it can be applied to our lives. This gives us the ability to share our concerns and doubts and have the support of other Christians to get us through those times. We can share how God has influenced our own lives and how others should put more faith in how He will get them through their struggles.

Having fellow Christians to have fellowship with, helps to keep us accountable for our actions. If we slip, they will help reel us back into how we should live. You need this regular conversation with those with the same faith to help develop your faith to a higher level. The more that we are conscientiously aware of how we interact with others, both personal and in business, in being true to our religious values, the more successful we will be.

Regular Bible study helps to keep your faith as a priority in your life and develop areas of yourself based on what you are reading. There are plenty of resources for doing this. There are daily devotions that will give you a different topic each day to reflect on. Some people read a little part of the Bible each day until they get through all of it. I, sometimes, look up a topic that I want direction on in the index of my Bible to find verses specifically about that topic.  Figure out what works for you and use it.

Have regular conversations with God throughout the day.  Prayer does not have to be when you wake up or when you go to bed and you are kneeling by the side of the bed or just before meals.

## *1 Thessalonians 5:16-18* *(NKJV)*

*Rejoice always, pray without ceasing, in everything give thanks; for this is the will of God in Christ Jesus for you.*

As your day goes by, thank God for what He is doing in your life at the time.  You need to understand that praying without ceasing means that you have that continuous conversation with God throughout the day.  As I approach a stressful situation, I ask God to help me get through it.  This may start with your morning commute.

I consider the application of your faith in how you give back to your friends, family and community to be your dessert. It is the last part of the meal. It is where you put what you learned and believe in into practice. All of us have talents strengths and need to use those talents to show God's love to others. There are many opportunities within your church community to volunteer your services. It should not stop there. Your faith in God should show through in your actions at work as well.

I have heard people say that they feel they have to leave their Christian values at the front door when they get to work. They do not believe that you can run a business without compromising some of your standards that you developed by having faith in God. This is far from the truth. I explain this in much more detail in my book, Faith Guided Leadership.

I do not believe that you can apply your faith to its potential by taking the ala carte' approach to your walk with Christ. You need to order and enjoy the four course meal. You will not have any regrets. What are you currently doing in your life to expand your religious experience?

How much **sense of control** do you have? Do you believe that you have control over the situation? If you believe that the choices that you make influence the outcome, then you have a better chance of dealing with it. You are not just throwing your hands up in the air in a sign of defeat. Every decision that you make affects the future. Some of these decisions have more of an impact than others. Sometimes it is years later when we see the impact. With other decisions, it is immediate.

How many times have you looked back at something that you did and had regrets? Think back of when you were a kid and your parents were scolding you for doing something that you knew was wrong. They probably asked you the question, "Why did you do ………..? Did you answer like most kids would, "I don't know."  Be aware of your decisions that you make and make them on purpose.  Stay true to your faith in God and the values that this faith represents.  Roy Disney said it well.

*"When your values are clear to you, making decisions becomes easier."*

I decided early in my career to put work in front of family. I moved all over the country without asking my spouse what she wanted. I did not take time off from work when my kids were born. I have regrets. The amount of stress that built up over the years played an impact on the outcome.  You cannot go back in time to change the decisions that you made. The sum of the decisions that you make in your life "is" your destiny. I am now single after two marriages partially due to my priorities earlier in life. The stress on the marriages played a factor.

Think about some of the decisions that you make every day. You have control, but sometimes do not realize it. You can control what situations you put yourself in that would increase your stress potential.

Do you have **control over your emotions**? You need to be able to see the signs of stress and know what works with your own body to control it. Everyone is different, so you need to know your own stress levels and recognize when you are getting elevated and can implement ways to reduce it. Think of your body as being a teapot sitting on the stove. It starts out having cool water in it. This is your body in a relaxed stage. What happens when the heat is turned up on the pot? The water inside of the pot starts to warm up.

This is like when your body is starting to react to a potentially stressful situation. You will start to see changes in your mood and your approach to everything around you. As the water in the pot gets hotter, small bubbles start to rise in the water. These are your warning signs that you need to be aware of. You need to take action to bring your stress levels back under control. If you do not, then the pot will be hot enough that the steam will make the teapot whistle. By then you have lost control temporarily of your stress level. Watch for your warning signs and turn down the heat.

Your **experiences over the years** will help you tremendously in this area. Take your career for example. The more experience that you have in your line of work makes you stronger. You know how to handle more situations as they arise.

This same scenario takes place in your potential stressful situations. Relate back to your experiences in how you calmed your stress levels in the past and it will help you get through your current situation. This allows you to be able to keep your composure and get through the situation.

# 5

# Causes of Stress

The situations and pressures that cause stress are sometimes referred to as *stressors*. We usually think of stressors as being negative, such as a major project at work with a tough deadline. Going through a divorce or major illnesses with a family member are stressors. However, anything that puts high demands on you or forces you to change your plans can be stressful. This includes positive events such as getting married, buying a house, sending kids to college, or changing jobs.

I discussed earlier about your attitude. Being an optimist or a pessimist will affect whether each of these scenarios will cause stress or not. Some things that cause stress in your life may not even affect another person, while they cannot handle situations that you consider normal.

There are many life changes that play a factor on our stress levels. As you go through the list, think about the items that apply to your life lately. This is a sampling of situations that will add potential stress to your life.  The more items that apply to you means that there is a greater potential for even more stress.   These include, but are not limited to the following:

Death in family

Marriage

Moving away from home for the first time

Promotions at work

Losing a job

Financial problems

Health issues for yourself or a loved one

Divorce

Changing jobs

Birth of a child

Starting college

Look through this list again.  Do you see something that most of them have in common?  Most of these involve change in your life. We like to get comfortable in our situation and change disturbs this. I am not saying that change is a bad thing. Change brings unexpected circumstances. It is the uncertainty that produces stress.

Notice that all of these are not negative situations. Marriage, promotions at work, and the birth of a child are a few that are exciting positive events in our lives. They all create change in our lifestyle and our daily routines. If you are aware of how you react to this change, it makes it easier to control the stress.

Not all stress is caused by external factors. Stress can also be self imposed. It is sometimes our own attitudes or approaches to situations that are causing our stress. Here are some examples:

Perfectionism

Unrealistic goals

Inability to accept change

Pessimism

Self doubt

What causes your stress? Everyone handles situations differently. What causes your stress may not even faze someone else. I have been in food service management for over 30 years. I have gone out to eat with people that are never satisfied with their food. There is always something wrong with their meal. I have been embarrassed at times with the pickiness and the quick reaction to send food back to have it made again. I rarely complain about a meal.

That does not mean that I accept poor quality out of my staff when they are serving guests. It changes the experience of the other guests at the table when you return your food and they have to uncomfortably eat theirs while you sit there and wait for a replacement meal. I do not stress over minor details of my meal enough to send it back. I do not want to inconvenience the other people that are enjoying the meal with me. Others really let it bother them and their stress level takes over in their decision to send the food back.

I struggle with going into a crowded room of strangers and starting up conversations with people. It raises my stress level. It is not my comfort zone. I can stand up in front of the same group of people and give a presentation and feel very relaxed. Others will be just the opposite. They are great at mingling, but scared to death of speaking to a group. Everyone is different and things will affect them differently than others. This is why it is crucial to learn your own stressors and how to control their effect on you.

Recently, I attended an open house at a friend's house. I helped out throughout the evening with the catering of the food. When I was ready to leave, the hostess felt bad about the fact that I was helping out. I explained that it was actually a tactic on my part to keep my stress level down. I did not know most of the people attending, but wanted to be able to mingle and blend in. By me helping hand out drinks or pick up empty plates, it gave me a reason to speak to people. It made for an enjoyable evening. You need to learn how to reduce the stress in aspects of your life and apply them. It can turn that awkward and stressful situation into a relaxed and pleasant one.

I have a friend that always complains about soccer moms clogging up traffic dropping off their kids at school. Other people may not let the morning commute bother them because they are enjoying listening to their favorite music. I personally do not enjoy rush hour traffic. I have decided not to put myself in that situation. Our office opens at 7:30 a.m., but I choose to arrive before 7:00 a.m.

everyday just to avoid the traffic. This eliminates the stress at the beginning of the work day.

When you are aware of what causes your stress, it gives you the ability to put things in place to prevent the stress. If the stress still exists, you can use some of your stress reducing activities to keep it under control.

# 6

# Healthy Living

## Get active and moving

Ok, I will admit it. I tend to become a couch potato if I am not careful. That does not mean that you cannot have down time. My problem is that I have a desk job, so I need to get more active in the evenings and weekends. One of my best stress relievers is to go for a long walk. During the week, it may be 1 – 4 miles. On a Saturday, I like to go for a 3-6 mile walk. I use it to clear my head of the problems from the week. If I am walking on the greenway, I can enjoy nature in a tranquil environment.

You cannot go from being inactive to being very active in a short amount of time. You need to start slow and build on your momentum over time. It may be that you start to take the stairs instead of the elevator or go for a short walk in the evenings. Your body needs to get used to the increased amount of activity. Any increase in the amount of activity is better than where you were before.

Exercise in many forms is a great stress reliever. We do not, as a society, exercise as much as past generations. As kids growing up, I remember spending most of the time outside playing. You would stay outside until the street lights came on. That was your queue to go in. You did not have video games as a deterrent to going outside to play.

As we got into our late teens and early twenties, we still kept active with pick-up games of basketball or football. Why is it, as adults, we slow down so much? I understand that our bodies cannot play the sports that we used to as kids. You have to incorporate exercise into your routine each week. You will reap the benefits on your stress level as well as your overall health.

I have friends that are avid about going to the gym. That is where they can relieve the tension from the day or get in the right mindset at the beginning of the day. To some, this is their form of socializing. This becomes part of their motivation to keep going back. This physical exercise contributes to a healthier lifestyle. People that are healthier tend to have less stress. One of the contributing factors of stress is injury/illness. If you take care of your body, the less prone that you will be for injuries and illness.

Find out what you enjoy doing that keeps you active. Incorporate this into your weekly routine. You will reap the benefits in the long run.

## Develop good eating habits

Eat small and frequent meals. This helps to keep your blood sugar at a more steady level throughout the day. This helps keep you healthy, but also eliminates a stress factor. There is no quick fix to dieting. If you eat a well balanced diet and keep your portion controls intact, you will see a healthy outcome. Too often, people try to starve themselves throughout the day. This makes them irritable and it starts to increase their stress level.

Drink plenty of water. I do not mean in your tea, coffee, sodas, etc. I mean good old fashion plain water. We tend to drink more of everything but water when we become stressed. How many people do you know that have to have their morning cup(s) of coffee to function. There are others that get their morning addiction of caffeine through their favorite soda. The caffeine dehydrates you.

You also need to get your water intake from a good balance of fluids and items in your diet. Fruits and vegetables contain fluid that counts toward your daily goal. It used to be that it was recommended to drink 8 cups (8 fluid oz.) of water daily. There are too many factors that play a factor in how much water your body needs each day. The main key is to avoid being dehydrated. You should have something to drink handy throughout the day. If you are thirsty, it means that you have waited too long between fluid in-take. Even mild dehydration can drain your energy. This contributes to potential stress.

## Get enough sleep

Do you tend to burn the candle at both ends? Do you try to start the day off early and also stay up late at night to squeeze as much into your day as possible. Those people that do that tend to have higher stress levels. They try to do too much. Most people will honestly say that they are a morning person or a night person, but not both.

I had this discussion over lunch earlier this week with a couple of managers that I work with. One of them said that they knew someone that started their day around 4:00 am all the time. They arrive to work early and then start firing off e-mails as they get into their routine. She said that this just ruins it for the night people. Don't you just love having the latest in technologically advanced phones? Your phone starts to notify you early in the morning that others are getting work done and you are not. The same thing happens when someone is a night person and is up late sending out e-mails.

Why do we feel that we need to respond at that time? It is because our expectations have changed with the new technology advances. We used to be able to leave work at work. When we left the office, everyone would wait until the next day to get in touch with us to conduct business. If we went out for lunch, we could get away for an hour and forget about work. Now our phones keep ringing and our co-workers get upset when we do not answer immediately.

It is no wonder why we have more stress in our lives. You need to learn how to leave work at work once again. Get yourself 7-9 hours of sleep every night. If you are an early riser in the morning, then you need to go to bed earlier in the evening. My kids used to make fun of me going to bed by 9:00 pm every night. It is the only way that I can stay rested. Being tired just makes you more susceptible to stress.

Hopefully your work hours are conducive to your natural sleep patterns. That is why some high school kids really struggle with getting enough sleep. They are not tired at night and want to stay up late, but their class schedule in the morning dictates that they wake up early. Here are some ideas that can help you get the sleep that you need.

Establish consistent sleep and wake schedules including on the weekends

Do not eat within a couple hours of bedtime

Do not drink alcohol of caffeine close to bedtime

Develop a relaxation routine an hour before going to bed to assist in falling asleep sooner

Avoid watching television and playing video games in bed

Make sleeping a priority in your life, just like your fluid intake is that I discussed earlier. It plays a factor in how you perform throughout the day. Being tired will increase your stress level.

## Drink alcohol sparingly and avoid nicotine

Do you know people that use these things as a stress reliever? They have convinced themselves that it helps calm them down. This may be a temporary fix, but the effects if not used in moderation can outweigh, very quickly, the short term pleasures that they get. Just the alcohol itself is not necessarily what reduces the stress in the short term. Normally, we are participating in a relaxing activity when we drink alcohol. This could be going out to a bar with friends after work. Just the fact that you are getting together with friends has the relaxing effect on your stress level. Imagine going home and grabbing a beer and going out to the deck to rest and enjoy a beautiful evening outdoors. It is not the alcohol that is truly diminishing your stress level. It is the peaceful situation where you can enjoy nature.

If you continue to drink while in these relaxing settings, eventually you associate the alcohol consumption with the relaxation. This potentially turns into an addiction. Most people think of alcohol addiction as needing to drink so much that they are drunk. This may be one of the signs, but alcohol abuse can happen at other levels as well. Alcohol abuse leads to relationship problems, poor performance at work, legal and deadly issues associated with driving while under the influence. These start adding more stress to your life than you had before the drinking. Can you put yourself in relaxing situations without adding the alcohol? If you can, you would be much better off.

Nicotine intake has a cycle effect on your stress level. Those that smoke, say that they feel a sense of calming come over them when they have a cigarette. Nicotine is absorbed in your bloodstream and quickly goes to your brain. Your brain has temporary sensations of pleasure and satisfaction. The more you use nicotine; your brain cells become desensitized and need increased levels to get those feelings back. Those that smoke on a regular basis will tell you that they start to get stressed before they get their next cigarette. This becomes an endless cycle that becomes an addiction. I do not need to go into the other negative effects of nicotine on your health.

# 7

# Calm Yourself

Everyone deals with stress and its symptoms in a different way. You need to learn what works best for you. If you do not learn to control your stress, it is undeniably damaging. You can, however, do things to reduce its impact and cope with the symptoms.

You may feel like the stress factors in your life are out of your control, but you can always control the way you respond to it. Managing stress is all about taking charge of your thoughts, your emotions, your schedule, your environment, and the way you deal with problems. It also involves changing the stressful situation when you can and changing your reaction to it when you can't.

You can't completely eliminate stress from your life, but you can control how much it affects. Relaxation techniques such as yoga, meditation, and deep breathing exercises help you relax. A state of restfulness is the opposite of being stressed. When practiced regularly, these activities lead to a reduction in your everyday stress levels and a boost in your positive outlook. They also increase your ability to stay calm under pressure.

Learn how to get quick stress relief. Everybody has the power to reduce the impact of stress as it's happening in that moment. With practice, you can learn to spot stressors and stay in control when the pressure builds. It may be as simple as breathing exercises. Since breathing comes naturally, deep breathing is often overlooked as an exercise, but it's an excellent way to reduce stress.

Breathe in slowly and deeply. Be aware of the feeling of the air as it expands your lungs and your chest. You tend to have shortened breathes when you are stressed, so this exercise is to lengthen your breath. Hold it for 4-5 seconds. You are increasing the amount of oxygen that you are taking in. Then exhale slowly for 6-8 seconds to remove all of the stale air in your lungs. This gets rid of the carbon dioxide in your body. Repeat this for four times. When you feel stress coming on throughout the day, just take a moment to breathe. I picture in my mind a changing out of feelings. I am breathing in a new relaxed attitude and blowing out the stress that I am feeling at the moment. You should experience immediate relief from some of the stress level.

If you are like me, you are behind a desk all day. The pressure sometimes builds up and you need a break from it. Get up and stretch. Sometimes, just a walk around the building makes a difference. We tend to get so wrapped up in a project that we do not realize what it is doing to our stress levels. Take a quick break. Just going to a co-workers desk to ask them how their day is going will take your mind off of what is causing you stress.

Sometimes we are our worst enemy when it comes to building up our stress levels. We convince ourselves that the longer we continue to pound away at the project without a break, the sooner we will be able to put it behind us. As the stress level continues to build, though, the less productive we are. Take that much needed break and you will gain back the loss of time in productivity.

Meditation and relaxation techniques are especially beneficial when stress keeps you from getting a good night's sleep. I have a CD that I listen to when I have had a hard day and cannot relax enough to fall asleep. It takes me through a progressive body muscle relaxation. It starts with me concentrating on my toes and getting them to relax. It then works up to my feet, ankles, thighs and so on up my body to my shoulders and finally to the top of my head and alternatively down through my arms to my fingertips. By the time I get through the CD, I am very relaxed and at times have fallen asleep before it was over.

I have spoken to a lot of my friends and some feel that dancing is a great form of stress relief. This has worked for me except the first time that I tried to learn how to two step in Texas when I was on a blind date. I was stressed about not doing it right and ruining the date. Once that initial fear, and the stress that came with it, went away, I had a relaxing night. The key is to figure out what works for you. You need to learn what activities work best for reducing your stress level. Add that activity into your regular routine and watch how well it reduces your stress level.

Music has a relaxing effect on your body. We get wrapped up in the melodies and forget about what was bothering us. This helps us wind down on our commute back home at the end of a tough day at work. I listen to music from the 70's and I start thinking back to what I was doing when the song first became popular. Sometimes, I have to temporarily change the station when it brings up bad memories, but most of the time they are good.

To others, playing music is the calming source in their life. A good friend of mine enjoys relaxing in a rocking chair, playing his guitar, singing, and sipping sweet tea. You have to be from the south to really appreciate a good sweet tea. He feels that whatever stress the music does not get rid of will be drowned out by the sweet tea.

Another friend enjoys a long bicycle ride with friends. The exercise plays a factor on her stress levels along with the opportunity to spend time with friends. Socializing over a glass of wine is just icing on the cake at times.

Have you ever been absorbed in a good book and could not put it down? It is because you get absorbed into the story. You just want to read more. You tend to forget about your surroundings when this happens. It is hard to be stressed about what is going on at work when you get absorbed into a book. As a writer, the best compliment that I have received is when someone says that they could not put it down. They had to continue reading to find out more. Find yourself a big comfortable chair and a good book and experience the stress relief.

Others get the same result from video games. They get so involved in the game as a character and forget about their surroundings. Time quickly passes by and they forget about their stress.

I have a few friends that enjoy taking their motorcycles out for a ride. As one puts it, she loves seeing all of God's beauty and let her troubles go in the wind. Every one of us has areas of our lives that are a great stress reliever. The key is to be aware of what works and do these activities before our stress level gets out of control.

A stress reducer for a high school classmate of mine is a day at the shooting range. I saw a show on television the other night about guys at the shooting range with pumpkins. They "carved" out their jack-o-lantern faces with the bullets flying through the pumpkins. That seemed like quite an experience.

Both of my sons love playing guitar. One plays acoustic guitar and the other plays bass. I can witness how relaxed they are when they are playing. I recently bought a drum set for them to goof around on and try to learn how to play. It would be neat for me to learn how to play the drums. I always wanted to over the years. I could play the drums and they can play the guitars and we would have quite the band. All we would need is vocals.

I now know why it was best for me to play trumpet while in school. Trying to coordinate two feet and two hands doing different things at the same time is even worse than me trying to learn how to two step. I do not need that stress in my life, so will leave the drum set to the kids. The band idea will have to wait.

Prayer time has come up on many people's list of calming activities. One person said that she just sits still by her bed and becomes so still that she can hear from God. She gets still in her thoughts and spirit. Then a sense of peace and calmness comes over her. When you allow God to step into your daily life, He can play such a big factor in your stress level.

## "Bear one another's burdens and you will fulfill the law of Christ"

We have had the discussion in our Sunday school about how we, as Christians, need to be there for each other in times of need. The emotional support alone has a healing effect on us. In Galatians 6:2 it states "Bear one another's burdens and you will fulfill the law of Christ". As we see those around us in stressful situations, we need to lend our support. Sometimes it is just lending an ear for them to be able to vent. We can take a task off their plate to loosen their load.

We can help by providing some of our time. Habitat for Humanity is an organization that provides houses for people in need. Just donating a weekend of labor makes a huge impact on the recipient's life going forward. Volunteering is a great stress reducer. In many cases, it puts your struggles into perspective. You realize how blessed you really are.

We have volunteers in our church that participate in the Stephen Ministry. Stephen Ministry began in 1975 when the Rev. Kenneth C. Haugk, Ph.D., a pastor and clinical psychologist, trained nine members of his congregation in St. Louis to be *Stephen Ministers*. They assisted him in providing Christian care and support to people in his congregation and community who were experiencing life difficulties. The trained caregivers were so enthused about their ministry; they encouraged Dr. Haugk to offer *Stephen Ministry* to more congregations.

The name *Stephen* comes from St. Stephen, who was the first layperson commissioned by the Apostles to provide caring ministry to those in need (Acts 6). More than 11,000 congregations are enrolled in the Stephens Series. They represent more than 160 different Christian denominations and come from all 50 states, 10 Canadian provinces, and 24 other countries.

Stephen Ministers are not counselors. They are Christian caregivers. Their role is to listen and care – not to counsel or advice. It is a confidential ministry, so what a care receiver tells a Stephen Minister remains confidential. If you are struggling with life's circumstances and would like to find out what Stephen Ministry can do for you, please contact them through their website at www.stephenministries.org or call them at (314) 428-2600.

There are passages in the Bible like this one that let us know that God will handle our burdens in life.

## *Matthew 11:28* **(AKJV)**

*Come to me, all who labor and are heavy laden, and I will give you rest.*

I was speaking with a co-worker today about what she does when the tasks at hand get overwhelming. She said that she prays in the morning and at night. She takes care of what she has time and control over to be able to handle and gives God the rest to take care of. We tend to stress over what is beyond our control. We can learn from her approach.

I used to stress over getting ahead in my career. I was never going to be satisfied until I was promoted to the next higher position. I never was happy and content where I was. I always wanted more. I finally figured out that this attitude was part of what was causing the stress in my life. I prayed to God to have Him take over the control of my life. I quit trying to get promoted and just tried to do the best job in the position that I had.

It was not long after that when a new position opened up in our district office. It was an ideal position for me. I interviewed for the job and got it. God was taking care of me. My stress level immediately dropped. I no longer had the feeling that the only way that I would be happy was to get a higher up position in the company.

# 8

# Who is in Control?

Are you in control of stress or is stress controlling you? Part of the nature of stress is that the circumstances start to get out of your control. We like to have full control of the situations around us. This is not always possible. It is how you react to this lack of control that dictates your stress level.

When you feel agitated, do you know how to quickly calm yourself? I have given some examples already. What works for you? Do you put those techniques in practice at an early stage of the stress coming on? Are there others that you can turn to in times of stress? This could be co-workers or your best friend. Can you share with them your frustrations and their response is the calming factor?

Some people get very frustrated when stress increases. They turn to anger as a way to vent their stress. Does this describe you? If so, can you develop a technique to let go of the anger? This frustration and anger, many times starts with being impatient. As our population grows, so do the crowded highways, the longer lines in the stores and we cannot get things done as quickly as we want. This built up anger makes us a ticking time bomb for a heart attack. We have to learn anger management as a way to reduce our stress if we suffer in this area.

It is not surprising to know that many of the techniques for anger management are also used for stress management.

- Stop to breathe – During those tense moments, take a quick break and breathe. Long, slow breathes will help calm you and get you back into control.

- Express your frustration, but think before you speak. When dealing with an employee, you can describe why you are frustrated, but do not say things that are going to add fuel to the fire.

- Be respectful and specific when addressing the issues.

- Do not hold a grudge. Holding grudges will prevent you from thinking clearly. You will let things get out of perspective.

- Remember that you are trying to diffuse the anger as quickly as possible.

When you get home from work are you relaxed? If not, develop techniques along the way home that put you in the right state of mind. You need to be able to leave work at work. Realize that rush hour traffic does not always move at the same pace every day. If you let the fact that it took you 15-30 minutes longer to get home increase your stress level, think about the people that were involved in the accident that caused the back up to begin with. You are in a much better situation than they are. Count your blessings instead of your struggles and you will have less stress.

Gain control of your emotions by getting away from the situation causing the stress. Jesus did this according to Scripture in **Mark 6:31 (NLT)**

*Then Jesus said, "Let's go off by ourselves to a quiet place and rest awhile." He said this because there were so many people coming and going that Jesus and his apostles didn't even have time to eat.*

There are times in our lives where too many things are going on around us and we need to get away from it to be able to relax.

Too often, we want to have full control of our lives. If we let go and let God be in charge of our lives, we would live a less stressful life. It all starts with prayer. We need to talk to God on a regular basis to help us through life.

How often have you asked God why something happened to you? Our lives are one like big puzzle. When I was growing up, I loved working jigsaw puzzles. At the beginning, you would lay out all of the pieces and start by finding the pieces with a straight side. That is how you would build the border of the puzzle. You look for like colors that may go together. It is not until you are further along that you start to gain speed. As you see the picture developing in front of you, you can tell where some of the pieces fit in.

You have the advantage of having the picture on the box cover so you know what the end result will be. In life, though, we do not know the end result. Sure, we can create some of our own destiny by the decisions that we make. When you decide to pursue a college degree, you have the ability to choose the type of career that you are training for.

There are many outside influences that may change your plans. Only God knows the full picture of your life. The puzzle pieces are the different circumstances in your life. These range from your accomplishments to the struggles. Too often we take credit for the accomplishments in our lives and blame others, or God, for the struggles. The time that you missed that green light when you were in a hurry, may have prevented you from getting into an accident further along in your travel that day.

Think about those that, though an accident or illness, were paralyzed and went on to a fulfilling life and witness to the good things that God has done in their lives. Our struggles are part of who we are. They are part of the jigsaw puzzle. If we just looked at the joys in our lives, we would not be looking at the full picture. I have no idea what God has in store for me. I do, though, have complete confidence that His will is much better than mine.

It is this confidence that allows me to not stress over what goes on in my life. I know that God will walk me through everything that I run into. If I have tough times, they will just build my character based on how I handle them.

Instead of worrying over our problems, further compounding our anxiety and stress, the Bible recommends taking everything to God in prayer. This verse in Philippians offers the comforting promise that as we pray, our minds will be protected by a peace that goes beyond our ability to understand.

## Philippians 4:6-7 (NIV)

*Do not be anxious about anything, but in everything, by prayer and petition, with thanksgiving, present your requests to God. And the peace of God, which transcends all understanding, will guard your hearts and your minds in Christ Jesus.*

It seems so easy. Why is it so hard for us to let go of our struggles and give them to God to take care of? We hate giving up control. Too often when we do pray it is for what we want instead of what God wants. I have been guilty of this. If we pray for strength to get through the situations, we would be better off. Some of these struggles are learning experiences for later on in life. I have had so many of these learning experiences that I was compelled to write a book.

God wants us to pray without ceasing. This has been a subject of many conversations between Christians. What does it mean? If you consider prayer as bowing your head, closing your eyes, folding your hands and asking God for things in your life, then you would be wondering how you can do that all the time. If I did that, I could not get anything else done. Some people pray in their cars on the way to work. That would be a way to multi-task and keep praying, but what happens when you get to work and have to concentrate on the tasks at hand?

I have friends that have regular conversations with God throughout the day. I try to do this, but get wrapped up in what is going on and forget about the conversation. I try to recognize things that I can praise God for. With this attitude, it is amazing how many blessing you really have in life. I may not have all of the material things that others have. I do, however, have many blessings that some people long for. When I start to struggle, I ask for strength to get through the situations. I do a decent job of talking to God throughout the day, but I do not pray without ceasing. I still have a long way to go in my walk with Christ, but know that He is there by my side.

Jean, a dear friend, says that she prays for a parking place when she goes to the store. I told her once that I thought it was taking it too far. Why pray for something that small. She reminded me that nothing is too small in God's mind. I pray for a parking place at times and it does not work for me. I then remember that I need to pray for God's will. God's will is probably that I lose some of this excess weight, so He opens a parking space further out so I have to walk. I always think of Jean when I am looking for a parking space. It reminds me of the fact that I need to talk to God more often.

We discussed this subject in Sunday school this morning. We have a member of our class, Angie that always has stories from her parents that teach you how to relate God's message in terms you can understand. Jesus spoke in parables and Angie's dad's stories relate the Bible to us in the form of a story as well. Here is how her mom explained endless prayer to Angie growing up. Most of us that have kids have used a baby monitor when our kids were young. One monitor is put in the room with the child. The other can be kept in another room or carried around the house by the parent.

You can monitor everything that goes on the room and can hear if the child is in need of anything. In some models, if you hear the child stirring, you can speak to them through the monitor to comfort them. If they start crying, you know that you may need to step into the room to handle their needs. Praying without ceasing is like the baby monitor. God can listen in on our lives at all times, even when we are unaware of his presence. It is like a continual conversation. Sometimes, we do more talking. Other times, He does more listening. He is always there for us. He can step in at any time in our lives.

We need to be more aware of the presence of The Lord in our lives. We need to make Him a bigger part of our lives. It needs to be more of a two way conversation. If you know me well, you know that I do not believe in coincidences. It is God's will playing out. We just need to be more aware of it so that we can really appreciate it.

I had talked earlier about how everyone is put in stressful situations and our stress level is dictated by how we handle ourselves in those situations. Another friend of mine, Mary, told me to put it into a three step process.

## Name it

## Claim it

# Tame it

You cannot address what is stressing you unless you know what it is. This is the "name it" step. Sometimes this is not what is on the surface. Here is an example. You had a heated argument with your spouse over breakfast before you left for work. You stormed out of the house just to get away and went in to work a little early. Later that morning, when someone brings you some extra work with a short deadline, you get very agitated.

It appears that you may be stressed over the extra work, but in actuality, you are stressed over the personal problems at home. When you name it, you acknowledge that this is what is causing your stress.

The next step is to "claim it." She described it to me this way. We are responsible for our own stress in some form or another. Take responsibility for what caused your stress. Claim it as your own. That is the only way that it will be important enough to you to take care of. As long as we consider it someone else's problem, we will not address it. We blame so much of our stress on those around us. We need to take responsibility of our own actions and our own stress.

The final step is to "tame it." Calm down the stress factor. You know what caused it. You determined what your role was in building up this stress. Now you need to take control of it. What can you do in the example that I used earlier? Make a phone call to your spouse and apologize for letting the argument get out of control. Explain that you were in the wrong to storm out of the house instead of working through the situation. That will start you down the path to getting control of the stress level.

I had a few potential stressful weeks in February 2012. There were emotional situations that kept coming and I was feeling the strain. It started out by being sick on my birthday with strep throat. That is not a good way to celebrate. I have an older truck that was my main mode of transportation. Our family had three other cars, but with my wife working a couple of jobs and two kids in college, it was not convenient when it broke down. I was coming home from the doctor's office after I found out that I had strep throat and the truck had not been running very smooth. Since I would not need the truck to get to work the next two days, I thought that it would be a good time to take it to the shop. They gave me the diagnosis that I did not want to hear. I needed a new engine.

About a week later, I found out that a friend of mine had a possible stroke and was having seizures and a temporary loss in the ability to speak. I added him to my prayer list. It was the following week that I received a phone call from another friend informing me that her daughter was killed that morning by a drunk driver. She was devastated and I was beyond words. The prayers started to turn into questions of why.

Later that month, one more of my friends called me to let me know that her mom was diagnosed with cancer. With what was going on in three of my friends lives, I realized that my truck issue was minor in the overall scheme of life. I thought long and hard about who was truly in control. It is not any of us on earth. God has a plan for us. It may take years for us to see it, but everything happens for a reason. My prayers changed to asking God to comfort us and guide us through whatever He has planned for us. I prayed for healing of the body and of the minds of all of my friends and their families. It gave me peace.

This does not mean that the situations are all of a sudden exactly how we want them. It meant that we would have the strength to endure the hardships that we faced.

# 9

## Put it in the Box

Do you get obsessed with the things that stress you? Have you been told to leave your personal issues at home and concentrate on work? We tend to carry "our baggage" with us wherever we go. When something is really bothering us, we cannot get it off our mind. We lose our concentration on what we should be doing. It is human nature. Our minds cannot concentrate on more than one thing at a time. We can quickly bounce back and forth between thoughts, which allow us to multi-task to a certain degree. Ultimately, though, if we keep having the stressful thoughts bouncing back into our heads, we cannot give the other thoughts and actions enough attention.

Picture, in your mind, a box that is small enough to hold in your hands but is big enough to hold a lot of small items. It may be a shoe box. It may be something a little bigger with a latch on it to keep it securely closed. The type of box does not matter. It is just to represent a part of your mind that you are going to place things in. This is where you are going to store your stressful items until you are ready to tackle them. There are many situations in our lives that cannot be resolved immediately or on the terms that we want. I would love to be able to take any issue and have it put behind me immediately so I can move on in life. This is unrealistic to think that it is possible. Some things are just going to take time to work themselves out.

It may be that you are waiting to hear back from an interview for a job that you really want. If you keep thinking about it throughout the day, you will become obsessed and lose your concentration. By you thinking about it continuously, it does not change anything. It does not make the person that interviewed you make their decision any quicker. All it does is increase your stress. I suggest that you "put it in the box". I am not saying that this will make the stress go away long term. It allows you the ability to schedule when you are going to deal with the situation.

Determine when you will open the box again to address the concerns. This may be in two days when the interviewer said that they would make their decision. At that point, you open the box and pull out that stress factor. You can then decide to make a phone call to determine of you got the job or not. You just saved yourself a couple days of stress over something that was not in your control.

It may be a situation where you need to drive to a business across town to resolve whatever is stressing you. You cannot take time off of work to go there in the morning, but it is tugging away at your attention. Visualize putting this stressor in the box to deal with later. When you have the ability to address it after work, then it is ok to pull it back out of the box.

The more that you let things bother you that you cannot change at that moment in time is what creates greater stress in your life. You need to learn how to set these things aside and concentrate on whatever task it is that you are doing. This principle can be applied to your home life as well as your work life.

# 10

# A Balancing Act

We live in a fast paced society. It is a balancing act to keep up all of the activities and not go overboard and create stress. The hours that we work keep creeping up. You may still be able to keep the hours at the office to 50 hours or less, but have you really added up all of the time that your mind is on work during your "off" hours. With the advances in the cell phone industry, we are working more than ever outside of our regular work schedule.

The cell phone sounds its annoying tone saying you have another e-mail. Years ago, you would not realize that an e-mail had come in or even care. Now we feel obligated to read it. We feel that once we read it, we might as well act on it. Your customers should understand that you need "down time". Why do you feel obligated to act on requests 24 hours a day?

You should be able to ignore the e-mails in the evenings. Rarely is it ever anything that just has to be taken care of. Not everyone works daytime hours, so there can be e-mails coming in during the evening.  These people are probably answering some of the e-mails that you sent during your normal shift.

I know that you have witnessed individuals that answer their phones when they are in the restroom. Why can't they draw the line on when to ignore the ringing of the phone?  They are out of balance. These are the people that live with continuing stress levels. You need to be able to "turn off" work.

I know that it would be hard to go from never ignoring the phone and the e-mails to being completely off work when out of the office.  Start with baby steps.  It may start with leaving the phone in your car when you go out to dinner with your family. That way, there is no way that you can be tempted to sneak a peek at it under the table.  If you are that addicted, you can look at it after dinner.  Enjoy the time with your family and give them your attention.  It will do wonders for your stress level and you do not get the opportunity to relive these moments with your family.  It is unfair to them to not have your full attention.

We miss out on so many opportunities to relax and de-stress because we do not have balance in our priorities.  I understand that our jobs are important because that is what pays the bills. We get lured by the feeling that making more money will make us happier. We see the rich and famous going through the same struggles as we do. They stress over money and relationships. It shows that just because you have money does not mean that you do not have struggles and the stress that goes with it.

You need to learn how to live within your means. Your relationships should not be compromised because of your desire to make more money. Give your career 100% during your work hours. When you get home from work, give your spouse and kids 100% as well. When was the last time that you played a game with your kids? When I was a kid, it was board games and cards that got the family together. Now, it might be video games that take the place for indoor entertainment for families.

When my kids were growing up, we loved to strike up a game of kick ball with the neighborhood kids. If we got a lot of the family together on vacations, we would have siblings, cousins, aunts and uncles all battling it out for the victory. How can you have any stress in your life at that moment? Too often, we do not find that balance between personal time and work time.

Sports can be a great stress reliever at all ages. Sure, our sports change as we get older. I decided when I broke my wrist playing touch football with my teenage son and his friends a few years ago, that it was time to re-evaluate my ability to compete at that level. I find it very relaxing to play golf. Note that I did not say that it was completely stress free and you would know why if you saw how I golf. I can say that I lose most of the stress of what was on my mind going into the round of golf.

Find what activities give you the stress relief that you need. Going for a long walk is a method that is used by many people. Put the phone on silent if you feel obligated to take it with you in case of emergency. I do not mean vibrate mode. That does not mean silent because it still causes you to react when it goes off.

I have talked to friends that say that worshipping at church is their way to reduce stress. It lets them concentrate on the blessing in their lives. They can also let some of the stress go by praying. That reminds me of a time during a church service that it was very quiet and someone's cell phone started ringing. My first reaction was "Why do they not have it in silent mode?" It was quickly followed up by laughter throughout the church because the ring tone was the song "The devil went down to Georgia."

So far I have talked about work being the cause of stress and personal time as our relaxation time. This is not necessarily so in all cases. Take, for example, someone taking care of an elderly parent or sick relative. As soon as they get home, there is no time to relax. The care that they give to the other person causes stress on them. I am not saying that they do not love them or that they want to change the situation. They just do not get that "down time" that can help them relax. It may be less stressful for them to go to work and have a caregiver taking care of them during this time.

Being at work gives them something else to think about and that is relaxing. You have to find a balance in your schedule to be able to handle the stressful situations and to have your relaxation time. Most people need personal time. The time that you are by yourself and doing what you love to do. Many people love to read books because it takes them into the story so much that they lose track of all the stresses of the day. Maybe you knit, scrapbook or love to paint. Find that activity and make sure that you schedule it into your week.

Our pets can give us a tremendous amount of stress relief. Through the process of writing this book, I did a lot of journaling. It was nothing formal. I would write down random thoughts in regards to stress management that I knew that I would probably want to put in this book. While reading one page of the journal tonight, I came across what I wrote one night in late March. "Sitting here journaling, Zoey at my side. (Zoey was our Chihuahua) As I relax, I start noticing more things around me. I feel her body move as she breathes. A dog is man's best friend. This is relaxing companionship." Zoey was tragically hit by a car in front of our house a couple of weeks later and did not survive. I really do miss her.

Do not force yourself on your pets. If they want to be left alone, they will let you know. Meet them on their terms. It creates less stress for them and therefore, for you as well. I have a finicky cat that cannot stand to be picked up or held. Try it and when she draws blood from her claws, you will understand. I sit back and watch as my kids get scratched up trying to give the cat some attention.

I will give you one guess as to whose lap she comes to lay on. I will pet her, which she loves, but do not try to hold her. I meet her on her terms and now have a cat that loves to lie on my lap. This is so peaceful. As I mentioned earlier, my dog used to claim my lap as hers. Both of my cats have decided that my lap is fair game again, so a night hardly goes by without one, if not both of them, on my lap.

We, as humans, need our peaceful times. This is where we find our comfort zones. These are our stress free zones. This may be snuggling with a partner watching a movie or just sitting in our favorite chair and reading a book. Keep your life in balance by scheduling the stress free activities in your life. They are just important to schedule as the other activities of our lives.

# 11

# What does your Schedule
# say about You?

You can control many of the things that stress you throughout the day by taking a hard look at your schedule. There are many instructors of time management out there. I have read about many of the techniques over the years. I cannot say that one method is better than another. The key is to find what works for you. I want you to be aware of how your time management plays a big factor in your stress level.

Let's start with the beginning of your day. Do you live and die by the snooze button? I know some people that set multiple alarm clocks and hit the snooze button a few times before ever getting out of bed. If you know that it will be 30-45 minutes after the first alarm to get up because you are tired, consider the fact that you just robbed yourself of 30-45 minutes of some of the best sleep of the night. You are normally in a deep sleep right before the alarm goes off. Just set the alarm for what time you want to ultimately get up and enjoy the last bit of deep sleep.

When my alarm goes off in the morning, I roll over, shut it off and turn on the television to watch the morning news. I lie in bed and watch the news for 15 minutes before I get up and get ready for work. This gives me the transitional period I need to become fully awake, while giving me the headlines of what is going on with the weather, etc. If I know that I am really tired because of some long work days or staying out later than normal, I just set the alarm 15 minutes later and get up immediately when the alarm goes off. I bypass the news and get on with my day. You need the proper amount of sleep to be able to keep your stress levels intact.

What time do you go into work each day? Do you have it timed so that you know if you leave at one time, you will get there 10 minutes early, but waiting 5 minutes make you late to work? Are you the one that tries to narrow that gap to where you can wait even longer to leave the house? You have just set yourself up for the first stressful moment of your day. You are the one that swerves in and out of traffic during rush hour and has road rage. It does not need to start that way. I have a gal that works for me that has a long commute each day. It is on the worst stretch of highway in Nashville for morning accidents.

She beats the potential stress by leaving her house early each day. She brings her kindle with her, so when she arrives early to work, she can read a book while waiting to clock in. If traffic is bad, she still makes it to work on time.

There are others that I know that will continue to complain about soccer moms taking their kids to school in their SUVs. Guess what. School starts the same time every day. Schedule your commute around it and that stress can be avoided.

How much do you squeeze into your schedule each day? Do you have a long "to do" list on a legal pad that goes on and on and on? Do you have the expectation that you will get through all of it today? Are you the person that has back to back appointments throughout the day and that will hold you on task to complete what needs to be done? Let's take a look at each scenario separately from a stress level point of view.

Your "to do" list is overwhelming. If you are not careful, you will get bogged down and stress will take over. Your tendency is to think about too many tasks at once and lose your productivity.

Decide what major tasks need to be tackled today. You need to work on one of the longer tasks. I have mentioned the need to take a break off and on throughout the day. When you do this, before getting back to the big project, knock out a couple of the easy ones. It gives your brain a chance to recharge before going back to the more time consuming task. It keeps your mind fresh. Realize that not everything will be completed that day and that is ok. Set realistic goals of what you can accomplish in a shift.

I have worked with people that have scheduled so many appointments throughout the day that mid-afternoon comes and they realize that they never scheduled lunch. You need to schedule breaks in your schedule. There will always be meetings that run over. There will be traffic slowdowns that delay you making it to all of your appointments in the short amount of time that you allowed. Allow extra time in getting to appointments. If you consistently show up for appointments early, you will be rewarded with less stress and also run across people that will see you early. This just gives your schedule even more flexibility to keep the stress down. Take something to read in the lobby as you are waiting for your appointment. It may be that business journal that you have a hard time finding time to read.

You should never put yourself in a situation that requires you to rush between appointments. That is just a recipe for stress. I have a tendency to eat lunch at my desk. I convince myself that I do not have time to stop for lunch. If I look at what I actually accomplish while trying to eat lunch, it is not very much. I am fooling myself. It would be much better for me to take my lunch into the break room and eat it there. It also gives me time to socialize with co-workers. There is so much less stress involved in taking that break. I will be more relaxed when I get back to my desk after lunch and will make up the "lost time" quickly.

Before you go home at the end of the day, plot out how your morning will start. I review the whole day, but mainly concentrate on the first couple of hours of my day. I lay out the projects that need my immediate attention. That way, when I get in to work in the morning, I can get right to work. If the tasks are greater than normal, I have two options. One is to stay a little later to get a jump start on them. The other, which is my first choice, is to come to work early to get it done. Coming in early to work allows me to avoid all rush hour traffic and to get a great deal of work done before the office really kicks into gear as other come in to work.

Your schedule has a direct impact on your stress levels each day. What are you going to do to reduce your stress level? Put it in your schedule. Schedule the stress relieving activity. It may be that you take a walk as part of your lunch break. Schedule time to get outside and play with your kids. This is a great activity for reducing stress. It takes your mind off of the stress of the day and builds the relationship with your kids. They will love you for it.

# 12

# Get Rid of the Clutter

We all hoard some things in our lives. Think about when you first moved into your house or apartment. Now look at what you have now in the same space. Are you amazed at how much extra "stuff" you have accumulated? I had to add shelves in my garage recently just to be able to squeeze one car into my two car garage. I should have thrown out more items than I did.

We tend to not get rid of things in our lives. We hold on to memories with some of the items. We keep an extra half of a closet of clothes because we may be that weight again, or we think that we "may" wear that outfit again. Next thing you know, it is out of style. We still do not get rid of it. Why is that? Normally it is because the clutter does not really bother us or get in the way.

Do you participate in the act of "spring cleaning"? It is that annual task of trying to get rid of the excess things around the house and organizing what is left. Then you give it a thorough cleaning. We need to take this approach to other areas of our life other than just the physical items. What if we uncluttered our relationships? I have a friend that called me recently and was frustrated with another long time friend of hers. She was obviously stressed over their relationship lately. Sometimes, we hang on to relationships longer than we should. I know that it sounds cold and heartless, but hear me out. As we get older, we change in what we believe in and how we act. If you have friends that are still living a partying lifestyle like in their twenties and you have put those years far behind you, then you are probably not as compatible as you used to be.

I am not saying that you quit being friends with them, but your relationship may start to grow apart and that will help you reduce your stress. Fill that gap with people that are more similar to where you are now in your life. Sometimes your friends become your clutter. People do not work for the same company for 30 or more years anymore like they used to. You will probably have multiple jobs and possibly multiple careers over your lifetime. Do not let your old jobs become clutter. You need to move on and not dwell over the good and bad things of the previous job. Concentrate on where you are in your life and the future that your new job is going to take you.

You need to de-clutter your time commitments. I am guilty of committing to too many things in my life. I have found myself active in too many organizations and volunteered for too many things at church. I started finding my stress level increasing. I could not give an organization enough of my time and attention. I started to have to bypass certain obligations at church because they conflicted in time with other commitments. I finally had to step back and make some tough decisions. I had to step back down from being on a board of directors for an association because I did not feel that the time and effort that I gave them was as good as they deserved. When you over commit, you do not do things at 100%. I had found this to be the case.

I stepped back out of a volunteer position at church so that I did not have the scheduling conflicts anymore. I started to see my stress levels go back down again. You cannot keep up everything that you have done for years and just add to it. You eventually need to drop some things off to add more. That is ok.

Simplify your tasks throughout the day. Just walk into my office and you can see right away how much stress I have or do not have. All it takes is to look at my desk. If I have papers scattered all over my desk, my stress level is higher. When I have everything neatly organized and out of the way, my stress level is lower. I am bad about working on too many projects at once. I am working on a project and someone comes in and says "Can you do something for me? It will only take a minute." I normally put my project on hold and help them out. Next, my boss walks in and says that he needs some information for an upcoming meeting. I let him know that I am busy and will get to it very shortly. I lay down the notes in front of me. The phone rings and one more project is given to me that needs to be done. Did I mention that annoying e-mail pop up message telling me that I have new mail in my in-box?

Before I know it, I am bouncing around all of the tasks trying to figure out who to please first. The stress starts to build up. How could have I avoided this dilemma? The easiest two ways are to let the call go to voice mail and to shut off that e-mail pop up. You need to concentrate on the task at hand. You lose so much productivity when you start to bounce from task to task. Try as much as possible to work on one project at a time. When I am traveling to other offices, I am so much better at this. I let people know ahead of time that I will only be checking e-mail periodically throughout the day. When I do go into e-mail, I work on just getting the responses back that are needed and quick tasks tied to them, to be able to get back to whatever I was working on before doing e-mail.

There is nothing wrong with using voice mail to control your day? Did you know that they even put voice mail capabilities on cell phones? Some people do not realize that. They feel that if you have a cell phone you should be available 100% of the time. Take a close look at the personality of these people. I bet you see one thing in common with all of them. It is stress. To them, everything is a priority. You should drop everything to take care of what they need right now.

I lay my cell phones down on my desk at the beginning of the day. If I go into meetings, or go back to another department to discuss things with fellow team members I do not take the phones with me. It drives some people nuts. They expect me to always be available for their needs. I want to give 100% of my attention to the people that I am meeting with. I do not need the distractions. There has never been anything that could not wait until I got back to my desk to handle. That does not mean that all voice mails that are left are not urgent. Most though can be put off while you complete the task at hand.

You need to realize what is important in life and give them more of your attention. Try to remember that everything that is important is not always urgent and everything that is urgent is not always important. It is helpful that the more that we can clear our minds of the clutter, the more that we can look towards our long term vision. Use your stress eliminating techniques to clear your mind. This will allow you to concentrate on where you are going in life. It may be a personal or a career goal. It is important that the more that you can prevent yourself from being bogged down by the distractions, or clutter, in your life means that you can concentrate on your future.

# 13

## Reality Check

It is great to have a dream of living stress free, but let's face the facts. You will always be subject to stressful situations. The key is to develop control over how you handle these situations in your life. This will not happen over a short period of time. It is a journey that you must take. Your goal should be to always strive to get better. You should be able to look back at times in your life that you were put in a tough spot and compare how you handled it then to how you would handle it now.

There are some areas in your journey that a little stress is a good thing. Learn how to embrace these times and not let them take control over you and your emotions. Paul writes in the letter to the church in Rome.

### Romans 5:3-5 ESV

*Not only that, but we rejoice in our sufferings, knowing that suffering produces endurance, and endurance produces character, and character produces hope, and hope does not put us to shame, because God's love has been poured into our hearts through the Holy Spirit who has been given to us.*

Think back through your life and your experiences that have helped produce your character. Some of them have been stressful, I am sure. Knowing what you do now, how would you get through these same situations? Would it be easier and less stressful? Too often, we get wrapped up in the moment and think about all of the things that can go wrong. Why can't we just think about all of the things that can go right and rejoice in it?

I remember helping with a children's musical and how we worried about getting the lighting just right. It was very frustrating to not be able to figure out the control panel for the spot lights. We tried everything, with no luck. All we could think about was what it would be like to have areas of the stage with lower light levels than the rest. Finally, I had to convince myself that the parents in the audience were there to see their kids act and sing and praise The Lord with their musical. Their praises would be adored in any level of light. We forgot what was really important and stressed over something that we should not have. I look back at the experience now and can see that no one noticed or cared about the lights. Would have it been better with more lights? Yes, probably so, but did it take away from the experience without it? No.

Embrace your struggles instead of stressing over them. Remember what is truly important in life. Normally it is not what we put so much stress into. These struggles will only make you stronger in the end.

You can dream about having a stress free life, but the reality is that you will always have some stress. There are too many areas of our lives that have potential stress tied to them. There will always be loved ones that we worry about. It may be a parent struggling with a terminal illness or a teenager learning to drive a car for the first time. If you love them, it will cause stress in your life.

It reminds me of when I was learning to drive. My dad had taken me out for a drive one afternoon. It was the first time that I had the opportunity to drive on the highway. When you came to a curve, there would be a recommended speed limit for safely getting through the curve in the road. I was very cautious about following the posted speed limit. Dad commented that I could take most of the curves at 10 mph faster than the posted speed, so I started doing that.

We left the main highway and started taking back roads. I had never driven them before, so kept the same approach of taking curves at 10 mph faster than what was posted. That is when the "stress of having a teenager learning to drive" kicked in. I took a curve with a posted speed of 15 mph at 25. It was a 90 degree curve. Dad grabbed the steering wheel halfway through the turn. When we got through it, he asked me if I thought that we would make the corner and I confidently answered "yes." He said that he did not. We proceeded to drive straight home. When we got home, I heard him tell my mom in the other room that he was never going to take me to practice driving again. He would leave that up to the school system and the driver education course.

What you can do though is learn how to keep your stress to a manageable level. The key is to learn what causes the stress in your life. By learning this you can be proactive in keeping the stress levels down. Implement some of the techniques described in this book to keep you relaxed in these situations.

How are you going to get to the desirable level of stress in your life? There is no magic wand. You have to take steps along the way. Set a goal of improving one major area of stress in your life this month. Just being more aware of this one area will help you to take control of it. It may be that you simplify your schedule. Allow more time between appointments. Determine what meetings are truly essential and excuse yourself if possible on the ones that are just time drainers in your schedule.

If you are struggling financially, it puts quite the pressure on your relationships at home. It starts small and is like a snowball rolling down hill. You need to start with small steps. Awareness of everything that you spend money on is a key to success. There is probably money that you can save throughout the week that you never thought of in the past. As you see progress, your stress level will get back into control.

I cannot emphasize enough the need to have realistic goals when it comes to getting control over the stress in your life. It probably took a while to build up that much stress, so do not expect it to go away overnight. It takes a conscious effort of your part. I have discussed numerous ways to help relieve your stress. Add a few items into your routine. What works for others may not work for you, so determine what works and continue doing it.

# 15

# Summary of Stress Relievers

Here are some stress relief techniques that have been shared with me by my friends, family and co-workers.

Sitting in your favorite chair and reading a good book

Going for a walk

Relaxed breathing – slow deep breathes

Yoga

Laughter

Healthy eating

Exercise

Prayer

Bathtub full of bubbles, a glass of wine and some good mood music

Bike ride with friends followed by fellowship over food and drinks

Riding a motorcycle and seeing all God's beauty and let your troubles go in the wind

Sex

Playing guitar

Practicing shooting a basketball

Playing golf

Sitting still by the bed and becoming so still that I can hear from God.  Being still in thoughts and spirit when a peace and calmness comes over me

'72 Gibson SJ, a rocking chair and a glass of tea. I can sit, rock and sing most of my stress away. The rest I will drown in sweet tea.

A day at the shooting range

Journaling

Getting involved in your church

Helping others pays you back in blessings. Those blessings wash away some of the stress.

I draw on God to focus and get through this

Name it, claim it and tame it.  Learn what is causing the stress.  Determine how this has been brought on because of something that you did. Take control over it.

Stephen Ministry – participate or ask to have a Stephen minister meet with you.

Read the Bible

Going to the gym

Save for an emergency fund

Attend church

Leave for work earlier than you need to

Get plenty of sleep

Avoid excess alcohol

Quit smoking

Spend time with your pets

Ignore work e-mails at night

Do not take your cell phone in a restaurant

Well balanced diet

Playing video games

Have a conversation with God during a long walk

Playing sports

Playing games with your kids

Snuggling with your spouse while watching a movie

Count your blessings

Call your kids or your parents. Just having a conversation with those you love helps reduce stress

Clean and organize your house. Getting rid of the clutter in your life helps reduce your stress level

Relax on your deck and enjoy nature

Meditation. Sit in a place where you will have no distractions. Doing this in the evening for 15-30 minutes does wonders for inner peace and relaxation.

Progressive relaxation – focus on tensing and then relaxing all parts of your body starting with your feet and working your way up

Volunteer – it takes the focus off of you and puts your issues into perspective compared to others that you are helping

Stop procrastinating

Learn to say "No". otherwise you overload yourself trying to do too many things

Do aerobic exercises, a brisk walk or a run

Pet or play with your pet, but do it on their terms. Do not force them to do what you want to do

Woodworking

Play the piano

Listen to music

Having a good cry and letting all of your emotions out

Pray to God and begin new activities with a positive attitude

Daily devotionals

Martial arts

Do not use a credit card. Wait until you can afford something to buy it.

Meditation and breathing exercises

Vent with a close trustworthy friend

Chocolate, the cure all. Need I say more?

Go for an evening out with friends

Surround yourself with positive people and friends

Eat lunch in the break room and not at your desk

Take a scenic walk

Get a massage

Blowing stuff up on video games

Go for a swim

Work crossword puzzles

Drink plenty of water, not tea, coffee, sodas or energy drinks

Go to a movie

Go camping or hiking

Going dancing regardless of the style of music

Playing video games with your kids

Relax by painting

Take a nap. Too many times when we are stressed we are not getting enough sleep

Going fishing

Kick boxing

Riding horses

Start a new hobby or pursue your life-long dream

Pray a lot and realize that God is in control. Let things go and rest in that knowledge. Everything that happens is for a purpose

Look for the positives in all situations

Taking a hot bath with candles

# About the Author

Thomas Mayberry is a Christian writer dedicated to helping others to be successful by following their faith in God. He knows that the more that we let God be in control in our lives the better off we will be. His first book, Faith Guided Leadership, was published in September 2011. Part of being a good leader is to be able to establish a stress free work environment. This starts by taking control of your own stress levels.

Thomas has learned over the years the effects of stress in your life. It took bottoming out in depression built up by stress to learn what was truly important in life. His religious beliefs now dictate the way he leads people in business and everyday life. He is more aware of his stress levels than any other point in his life. Thomas wants to share what he has learned with you so that you can achieve the same success in your life.

Find out more about having Thomas speak to your group and to follow his blog by going to www.faithguidedleadership.com His first book, Faith Guided Leadership is available through Amazon.com.

Made in the USA
Lexington, KY
28 February 2013